THE KOREAN WAR

From World War to Cold War

Written by Quentin Convard
In collaboration with Thomas Jacquemin
Translated by Rebecca Neal

THE KOREAN WAR   1

Key information

Introduction

POLITICAL AND SOCIAL CONTEXT   3

The division of Korea

Whose decision was it to attack?

KEY PROTAGONISTS   8

Syngman Rhee, South Korean politician

Douglas MacArthur, American general

Harry S. Truman, American statesman

Kim Il-sung, North Korean military leader and statesman

ANALYSIS   16

The development of the conflict

The North Korean dawn invasion

The UN enters the war

The USA leads operations

The American landing at Inchon

The 38th parallel

The meeting between MacArthur and the President

China enters the war

Negotiations and the armistice

IMPACT   34

North Korea and South Korea

The USA and the UN

SUMMARY 36

FIND OUT MORE 39

THE KOREAN WAR

KEY INFORMATION

- **When:** 25 June 1950 – 27 July 1953.
- **Where:** Korea.
- **Context:** the Cold War (1945-1990).
- **Countries involved:** North Korea and its allies (China and the Soviet Union) against South Korea and the United Nations (mainly the USA).
- **Key protagonists:**
  - Syngman Rhee, South Korean politician (1875-1965)
  - Douglas MacArthur, American general (1880-1964)
  - Harry S. Truman, American statesman (1884-1972)
  - Kim Il-sung, North Korean military leader and statesman (1912-1994).
- **Outcome:** signature of an armistice with no real winner and recognition of two states.
- **Victims:**
  - North Korean side: 1.82 million military and civilian deaths, casualties and disappearances, according to some sources.
  - South Korean side: 1.55 million military and civilian deaths, casualties and disappearances according to some sources.

INTRODUCTION

The Korean War began as an internal conflict, before becoming global and pitting the Western Bloc and the Communist Bloc against one another. For three years, it gave an outlet to the opposition between East and West.

At 4am on 25 June 1950, Captain Dorrigo of the Korean Military Advisory Group was awoken by the sound of bombs: North Korea had just crossed the 38th parallel north, the imaginary border separating the two countries, and attacked its neighbour to the south. The military immediately sounded the alarm. A few weeks later, the USA entered the war against North Korea, led by General Douglas MacArthur, and the UN dispatched its armed forces for the first time since its creation. However, in February 1951, the war reached a stalemate. At the same time, negotiations took place between the Western and Communist sides, ultimately leading to an armistice in 1953.

Over 60 years later, Korea is still not unified and tensions remain high.

POLITICAL AND SOCIAL CONTEXT

THE DIVISION OF KOREA

On 15 August 1945, when Japan surrendered unconditionally to the winners of the Second World War (1939-1945), the Koreans, who had been under the domination of the Empire of Japan since 1910, were euphoric at the thought that they would finally have control over their own lives. Immediately, the Korean peninsula set itself the aim of forming a single large democracy which would bring together the North and South of the country. However, the USA, Great Britain and China had different plans for this small Asian country. At the Cairo Conference in 1943, these three countries recommended that Korea become free and independent again, but only in due course. This desire was reaffirmed and approved by the USSR at the Yalta Conference two years later.

As early as the Second World War, when the Soviets were taking part in the war between the Allies and Japan at the request of Franklin D. Roosevelt (American statesman, 1882-1945), it was agreed that the Russians and the Americans would share part of the peninsula. To do this, General Douglas MacArthur, a hero of the Pacific War (1941-1945) suggested dividing the country in two at the 38th parallel, which more or less corresponded to the middle of Korean territory. This arbitrary and artificial line, which crossed mountains that were over 2000 m high, did not take terrain, economy or society into account, resulting in some ludicrous situations. For example, one part of the city of Kaesong was in the Soviet sector, while the other part was under American jurisdiction. This imaginary border was not destined to last and originally was only meant to make it easier for the Soviets in the North and the Americans in the South to manage the surrender of the Japanese troops.

In 1946, a mixed Soviet and American commission was set up, and called on all democratic political bodies in Korea with the aim of forming a provisional government. However, due to the mounting tensions between the two great powers, the commission came to nothing. One year later, the USA brought the matter of the future of Korea before the United Nations, which decided to set up a new commission tasked with supervising the organisation of independent elections with a view to forming a government. However, the Soviet Union, which was hostile to the UN as it saw it as an organisation under the control of the Americans, refused to allow the commission to enter its occupied zone in Korea. The North therefore boycotted the elections and only the South was called to vote. Syngman Rhee was elected the first head of government in July 1948, and immediately afterwards the Republic of Korea was proclaimed, with Seoul as its capital. At the same time, the North of the country, with the support of the USSR, also organised elections. These elections, which were overseen by the USSR rather than the UN, resulted in a majority for the left-wing parties, who appointed Kim Il-sung, a former member of the resistance against the Japanese, as their leader. The North proclaimed itself independent and took the name Democratic People's Republic of Korea.

This dispute therefore resulted in two Koreas, each of which claimed to be the legitimate representative of the peninsula as a whole. The two new heads of state desperately wanted to reunite the country, but they both wanted to do this based on their own political ideology and were prepared to resort to arms if the situation required it. As such, all the conditions needed for a civil war to break out were in place, and only the presence of the two great powers could dissuade the Koreans from taking up arms. However, somewhat paradoxically, it was their absence and hostility that plunged the peninsula into a brutal war: in 1949, the American and Soviet troops withdrew within six months of one another, leaving behind some soldiers from both sides who were tasked with training the young Korean armies.

WHOSE DECISION WAS IT TO ATTACK?

Over 60 years after the end of the conflict, we still do not know who took the decision to attack and allowed the North Koreans to cross the 38th parallel, the starting point for the Korean War. Although it seems improbable that Joseph Stalin (Soviet statesman, 1879-1953) did not agree to – or at least allow – the attack, we cannot rule out Kim Il-sung's desire to confront the South. One thing is certain, however: the Soviet camp never suspected that this attack could have such far-reaching consequences and, above all, that the USA and the UN would enter the war.

Indeed, on 12 January 1950, the US Secretary of State Dean Acheson (1893-1971) announced that the American defensive perimeter extended from the Aleutian Islands to the north-west of the USA to the Ryukyu Islands (Japanese archipelago) in the Philippines. This excluded South Korea, a fact which was confirmed by MacArthur. Moscow then interpreted this careless statement as an invitation to invade Korea. Furthermore, at this time the Soviets underestimated the American army and thought that Washington was incapable of promptly dispatching an army to unknown territory. From their point of view, the USA possessed formidable atomic weaponry, but there were major gaps in its military capabilities, as its approach was deemed too traditional. Although this was the situation at the end of the Second World War, where scientists replaced foot soldiers, President Truman was gradually abandoning this tactic and had been building up a land army since April 1950. Finally, the Soviets knew that the USA was deeply suspicious of the new South Korean president, Syngman Rhee. The Soviet Bloc was not sure that Washington would take big risks to defend this head of state, who had been behaving almost dictatorially by violently repressing all Communist activity (there were almost 14 000 political prisoners in South Korea) and openly threatening to attack North Korea since his election. Furthermore, the USA refused to provide weaponry to South Korea, preferring instead to oversee and reserve the right to inspect its army.

However, the events that followed show just how mistaken the Communist Bloc was about America's intentions. The USA, for its part, was convinced that Moscow was stirring up rebellion in North Korea in order to tilt the balance in the Far East in its favour. In addition, the Republicans were still criticising Truman after the fiasco of the negotiations in China, which had seen the Communists come to power.

The president, keen to silence his critics, therefore decide to send American troops to Korea.

<u>DID YOU KNOW?</u>

China and the USA had maintained friendly relations since the late 19th century. However, when Japan was defeated in 1945, relations between the two countries deteriorated. When China split into two political camps, with nationalists on one side and Communists on the other, the USA decided to publicly lend its support to the nationalist Chiang Kai-shek (1887-1975). His opponent, the Communist Mao Zedong (1893-1976) interpreted this as a threat of war. The situation became even more explosive when Japan surrendered, as the Americans organised a sealift to help the nationalists take control of the major towns and cities before the Communists. Facing the threat of a civil war caused by the failure of negotiations between the two Chinese leaders, President Truman sent in General George Catlett Marshall (1880-1959) from 1945 to 1947 to try and defuse the situation. However, Marshall failed to reconcile the two parties and a civil war broke out. The Americans provided the nationalists with financial and material support, but the means they supplied were not enough to ensure victory. On 1 October 1949, Mao entered Beijing and proclaimed the creation of the People's Republic of China, which was recognised by the USSR and the Soviet Bloc countries, while Chiang Kai-shek fled to Taiwan.

KEY PROTAGONISTS

SYNGMAN RHEE, SOUTH KOREAN POLITICIAN

Portrait of Syngman Rhee.

Syngman Rhee was 75 years old when the Korean War broke

out in 1950. He was descended from royalty and joined the Independence Club, which was founded by a Korean journalist and politician with the aim of fighting politically against Japanese influence, in 1894. He was imprisoned for his ideas in 1897 and released in 1904, when he went into exile in the USA. He went on to obtain a PhD in his host country and led Korean nationalist opposition from Hawaii, where he had settled.

He returned to Korea when Japan surrendered in 1945, after 40 years in exile. He founded the National Association for the Rapid Realisation of Korean Independence, which won the 1948 elections, making him the first president of South Korea, proclaimed the Republic of Korea. Although he was patriotic and courageous, his authoritarian character and tyrannical conception of politics made the USA suspicious of him, especially when it came to weaponry.

After the end of the Korean War, Rhee was reelected four times. However, serious irregularities cast a shadow over his last electoral victory, and in 1960 a major popular uprising forced him to return to Hawaii, where he remained until his death in 1965.

DOUGLAS MACARTHUR, AMERICAN GENERAL

Portrait of Douglas MacArthur.

MacArthur, who had Scottish ancestry and was the son of a governor of the Philippines, was a renowned figure in the military. He graduated first in his class from the United States Military Academy at West Point in 1903, and was promoted to major in 1915 while fighting in France. In the 1930s he became Chief of Staff of the United States Army. After retiring in 1937, he was recalled to duty in 1941 and served in the Pacific, where he distinguished himself for two years by fighting in a number of battles. On 2 September 1945, he received the surrender of the Empire of Japan, and then served as proconsul to help the country to recover and return to democracy.

MacArthur, who famously said "You are remembered for the rules you break", thought that he was better placed than Truman to deal with questions involving Asia, and made it a point of honour to apply this dictum during the Korean War. He therefore had no qualms about flouting the orders of his superiors and the political authorities. In spite of his removal from command in April 1951 for straying from the rules and refusing to respect the hierarchy, he enjoyed high levels of popularity in the USA. Many people saw him as a future president, but he definitively retired from military life and died in 1964.

HARRY S. TRUMAN, AMERICAN STATESMAN

Truman giving his signature for the USA's involvement in the Korean War.

There was little to suggest that this judge from Jackson County, Missouri would become the 33rd President of the

United States, and even less that he would be the one to face challenges including the Second World War and the Korean War. Truman was a Democrat and was elected to the Senate in 1934, before being chosen as Franklin D. Roosevelt's vice-president. He held this post for 82 days, before replacing the President as leader of the country when Roosevelt died of a massive cerebral haemorrhage on 12 April 1945. Although he knew nothing of the Manhattan Project, which carried out research on the atomic bomb, he was the one who gave the order for it to be used to put an end to the Second World War, in this way ushering in the Atomic Age. He was elected in 1948, and his second term was mainly marked by the Korean War. His stances during the conflict, such as his decision to refer it to the UN, were initially viewed positively by the American public. However, when he removed MacArthur from his post, his popularity ratings plummeted and he was repeatedly attacked by Senators, who accused him of wanting to place the non-commissioned officers fighting in Korea in charge of the conflict. Despite the American victory, Truman failed to regain the trust of his fellow citizens, and this state of affairs persisted until the end of his presidency. When he left the Oval Office in 1953, he dedicated himself to writing his memoirs and took part in some campaigns to support Democratic candidates, before passing away on 5 December 1972 at the age of 88.

KIM IL-SUNG, NORTH KOREAN MILITARY LEADER AND STATESMAN

Portrait of Kim Il-sung.

Originally from the North Korean capital Pyongyang, Kim Il-sung was the founder and first leader of North Korea. He was elected in 1948, and was 38 years old when he decided to attack South Korea. In spite of his importance in Korean history, it is difficult to know exact details about his life because the huge cult surrounding him blurs the lines between reality and fiction.

We know that he joined the Communist Party in 1931 and was tasked with organising the popular revolutionary army which was fighting the Japanese occupier. His main feat of arms as a member of the resistance was the occupation of the town of Pochonbo (close to the Chinese border) in June 1937. He held the town for a day before fleeing and escaping from the Japanese police.

Although he is presented as a hero of the Second World War, his role in the conflict remains unclear. According to some sources, he played an important role in the Red Army during the Battle of Stalingrad (23 August 1942 – 2 February 1943). He was close to senior Communists, and was placed by the USSR at the head of the Provisional People's Committee for North Korea in 1946. After being elected as leader of North Korea in 1948, he made power in the country hereditary, allowing his son Kim Jong-Il (1942-2011) to succeed him following his death in 1994.

ANALYSIS

THE DEVELOPMENT OF THE CONFLICT

After a series of dawn raids which saw North Korea invade its neighbour in three days, the Americans gain control of the peninsula in a month, and then the Chinese drive back the Western forces in a few weeks, the situation stagnated and was at a stalemate for two years, before an armistice from which no real winner emerged was signed. Although the conflict featured some spectacular battles, such as the Second Battle of Seoul (22-25 September 1950) and the Battle of Inchon (15-28 September 1950), the fate of the country was initially decided at the UN, through a mixture of political negotiations, administrative ruses and diplomatic machinations.

Different sources give difference information concerning the forces present over the course of the war. It is nonetheless possible to estimate the number of soldiers engaged throughout the entire conflict. There were:

- almost a million Communist combatants, including:
  - 206 000 North Koreans
  - 780 000 Chinese
- 1.15 million South Korean and UN combatants, including:
  - 590 000 South Koreans
  - 480 000 Americans
  - 63 000 British

THE NORTH KOREAN DAWN INVASION

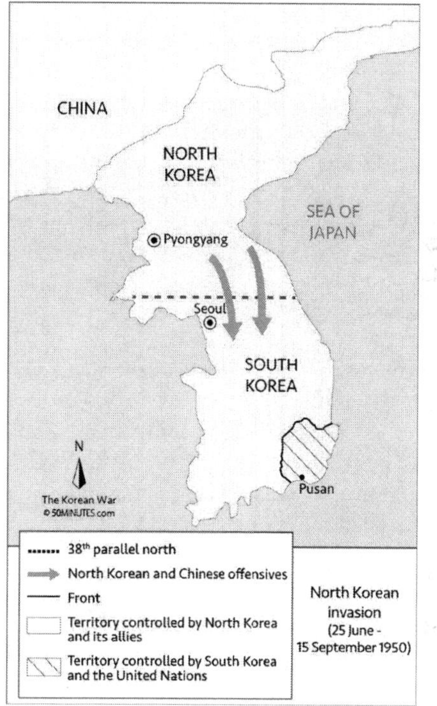

On the pretext of an alleged South Korean attack on the 38th parallel following the failure of the negotiations, the North Koreans decided to attack their Southern neighbours. Supported and equipped by the Soviets, who nonetheless did not officially commit to the war, the North Korean army crossed the imaginary border at dawn on 25 June 1950, without declaring war beforehand. The South Koreans faced the two corps of the North Korean army, comprising 138 000 men, with a small army of 38 000 soldiers spread across four divisions and one regiment, two thirds of whose members were on leave. Moreover, the North Koreans possessed substantial and powerful military equipment: 150 Soviet tanks, 1700 pieces of artillery and 200 fighter planes. Thanks to a well-prepared tactical approach which involved simultaneously attacking five strategic points, they easily overwhelmed the Southern resistance and quickly gained ground in South Korea.

The UN immediately called for a ceasefire, but this fell on deaf ears. The North continued its conquest, which it hoped would be quick, wanting to conclude its attack on 15 August, the fifth anniversary of independence. Kaesong, the former capital of Korea, which lay on the route connecting Pyongyang and Seoul, fell quickly under the tank offensive. General Chai's troops were now only around 20 miles from Seoul. At the same time, the Northern air force bombed the Kimpo airfield, which was located close to the capital and housed the aeroplanes of the South Korean army. The North Korean infantry ran into some difficulties in Chuncheon because the South Korean troops were all present there, and it could not rely on its tanks or its planes. Nonetheless, General Chai still had more men. He pressed on with the offensive and ultimately achieved his objectives: three days later, on the afternoon of 28 June, Seoul fell into the hands of the North Koreans.

THE UN ENTERS THE WAR

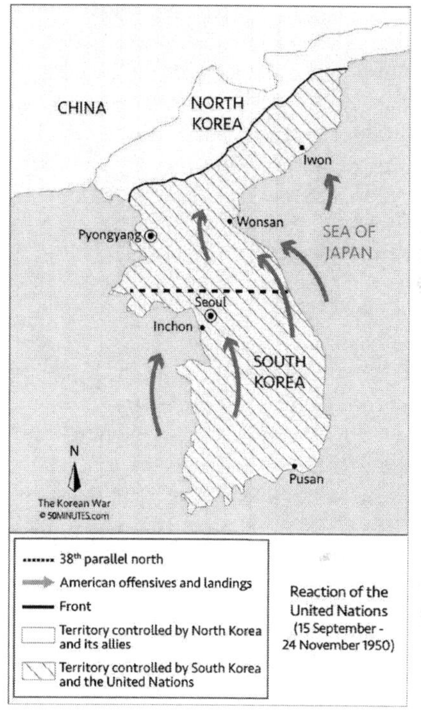

On 27 June 1950, at the request of the US delegate Warren Austin (1877-1962), the UN Security Council voted seven to one (Yugoslavia), with two abstentions (India and Egypt), in favour of the resolution asking UN member states to

provide substantial military support to South Korea in order to drive the invader back across the border. This vote was made possible by the fact that the USSR was boycotting the Security Council, as it was demanding that the West recognise the People's Republic of China and allow it to join the UN. The Soviets decided to stop attending sessions of the organisation until their demand was met, never imagining that the other countries would take advantage of the opportunity to pass the resolution.

The USA, for its part, did not wait for this decision before acting. As soon as he received news of the invasion, Truman gave the order to provide the government in Seoul with the weaponry it needed, which he had previously refused to do because of Rhee's aggressive character. On 27 June, before the vote of the Council, Truman delivered an address to the nation in which he announced his intentions and invited the USSR to extricate itself from the conflict and use its influence with North Korea to make it withdraw its troops. However, the USSR stood by the official version given by Pyongyang, according to which the South had been the first to open fire, and affirmed that it respected the policy of non-intervention.

On 29 June, Truman sent 33 000 men to the peninsula. They received the support of the UN Command created for the occasion on 7 July and headed by MacArthur. In addition, while the countries sitting at the UN each sent a contingent, American soldiers made up the bulk of the troops. It was therefore the US government rather than the UN that had tactical control over operations.

THE USA LEADS OPERATIONS

Hindered by the monsoon, a lack of knowledge of the region, the inexperience of its soldiers, the mountainous terrain and a lack of preparation, the American army initially sustained heavy defeats. Indeed, the soldiers, who mostly came from the fairly peaceful Japan, were not used to such conditions. The first battle, which took place in Osan, to the south of Seoul, ended in a complete rout for the Western forces, and when Taejon fell the American Major General William F. Dean (1899-1981) was taken prisoner. By the end of July, the situation was catastrophic: the UN troops only held the south-east corner of the peninsula.

On 10 August, the war began to develop in favour of the UN. While waiting for reinforcements, the American General Walton Walker (1889-1950) launched an offensive and North Korea was bombed heavily, cutting its supply lines. On 14 August, 500 tons of bombs rained down on Rason, the North Koreans' main supply base, just 17 miles from the Russian border. The North Koreans then had to retreat and abandon Daegu, followed by Pohang, which they had nonetheless relentlessly attacked. The UN soldiers managed to drive back the Northern troops and now had the opportunity to launch a counter-attack. As such, on 15 September, MacArthur opened a new front at Inchon, close to Seoul, giving his soldiers a stranglehold over the enemy armies. At least on paper, the choice to go through this city seemed wise: it was a stronghold of the Northern army and, once taken, would allow communications and supplies to the enemy army to be cut off. However, it was difficult to access and the Americans had no choice but to go via the sea and a channel to the East, which could easily be blocked. The undertaking was made even more difficult by the fact that the powerful current in the channel made navigation almost impossible. Furthermore, it was impossible to cast anchor in the sea and the port was surrounded by tall seawalls.

General MacArthur watches the bombardment of Inchon.

In spite of these myriad obstacles, MacArthur still decided to launch his operation, codenamed Operation Chromite, there. He thought that he would be able to use the difficulties to his advantage because the Koreans would not be expecting a landing there, but further south at Gunsan. Furthermore, MacArthur, who knew the region well, wanted to quickly lead a counter-offensive with the aim of stopping the campaign continuing into winter, which was reputed to be a particularly trying season in Korea. In order to prepare as effectively as possible for the landing, the CIA secretly dispatched troops to an island close to the port, in order to provide strategic information to the soldiers.

THE AMERICAN LANDING AT INCHON

The Americans landed in three locations:

- Green Beach, on the Island of Wolmido
- Red Beach, which surrounded Inchon
- Blue Beach, which also surrounded Inchon.

Fighting was fiercest at Green Beach. With an infantry battalion, around ten tanks, landing craft which had been used during the Second World War and aerial support which dropped napalm on the territory, the Americans conquered the island after six hours of fighting. The two other American attacks unfolded more smoothly and more quickly, which allowed the American soldiers to surround the peninsula and attack the North Koreans on two fronts.

Once the Battle of Inchon had been won, pressure from the UN intensified and the North Korean troops were forced to withdraw. Although many Northern soldiers fled or blended into the refugees, some resisted and took advantage of the confusion to take some towns in small groups and slow down the advance of the Western troops as much as possible. However, this resistance was short-lived: Seoul was recaptured on 28 September 1950 and, of the 130 000 North Korean soldiers enlisted, 100 000 would never return. At the start of October, the last North Korean units were destroyed at Uijeongbu.

American soldiers engaged in a street battle in Seoul in September 1950.

The Americans continued their advance to the north and crossed the 38th parallel on 10 October. Three days later, MacArthur had the city of Chongjin, a little under 40 miles from Manchuria, bombed for an entire day. This was one of the most important industrial centres in North Korea and, by attacking this stronghold close to the Chinese border, the general sent a strong message to the Communists. Immediately after this, Pyongyang was taken, and on 26 October UN troops reached the banks of the Yalu River (also called the Amnok River), which separates Manchuria from Korea, thus giving them control over the entire peninsula.

THE 38TH PARALLEL

Although the USA's primary mission was to drive the North Koreans back into their territory, the Western forces did not hesitate to cross the border. Galvanised by victory, the army did not stop to think about the potential consequences of such an action. Although initially no land expedition had been planned by the UN, a resolution was put before the General Assembly of the United Nations by eight allies of the USA stating that the priority was to ensure stability across the peninsula as a whole, by any means necessary, in this way implicitly authorising the troops to cross the 38th parallel and continue fighting beyond it.

On the back of his victory, MacArthur thought that it was essential to deal a fatal blow to Communism and erase the American defeat in China in 1949 by crossing the 38th parallel. In his eyes, victory would only be complete once the North Korean army had been wiped out. He therefore paid little attention to the threats made by China after the crossing of the 38th parallel.

THE MEETING BETWEEN MACARTHUR AND THE PRESIDENT

Once the 38th parallel had been crossed, relations between Truman and MacArthur deteriorated to such a point that the latter's removal seemed inevitable. He advocated an aggressive and brutal policy towards Communism, while the president, who was afraid of the conflict spreading to China, was trying to handle Beijing carefully. However, the main problem poisoning the relationship between the two men was the fact that MacArthur had no qualms about criticising the methods of his own government, even in public. He was, in effect, the strongman of Asia. Surrounded by a certain aura which he had earned during the battles he fought in the Pacific, he was the Proconsul of Japan and enjoyed a degree of freedom of action. In addition, he had been outside the USA for 14 years and was therefore out of touch with the reality of his country and with public opinion.

On 15 October, the President went to Wake Island to meet MacArthur. The idea of stripping him of his functions crossed his mind, but he wanted to avoid publicly dismissing him and making an enemy of this powerful man. Although this meeting was supposed to call MacArthur to order, at the same time it conferred on him additional prestige, as the President had come out to see him in person.

During the meeting, MacArthur apologised for his recent escapades, but remained firm in his position. In his eyes, Korea was already defeated and it was not in China's interests to send an army to defend it since it would be anticipating a major defeat. It was therefore time to finish the war and let the soldiers return home. Truman ended up agreeing to trust him, but reminded him that the president, not the military command, was responsible for matters of foreign policy.

CHINA ENTERS THE WAR

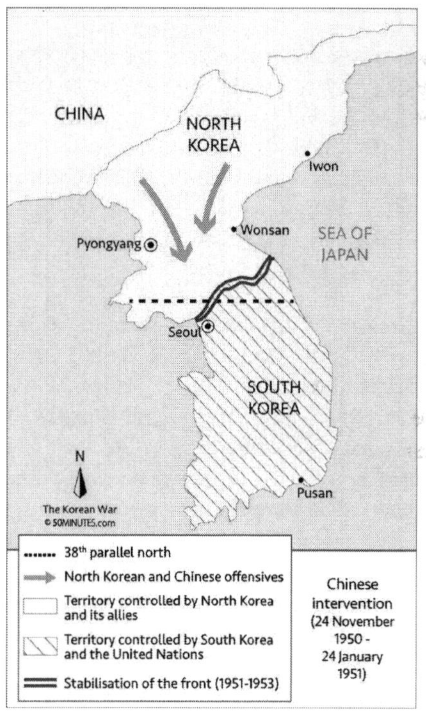

While the two American strongmen of the conflict were meeting for the first time, Chinese soldiers were quietly landing in Korea. This new invasion was only discovered some ten days later thanks to the capture of the first prisoners, and led to a resurgence of Communist guerrillas across the peninsula. Heterogenous groups of between ten and 1000 men laid mines and carried out raids on American facilities, making them a permanent threat. In addition, on 24 October, the Chinese deployed 200 000 men along the Yalu River, ready to intervene against the UN forces. However, it was on 31 October that the first fighting between Chinese and Americans soldiers really broke out. At the head of a sizeable army comprising 56 divisions, the Chinese commander Lin Biao (1907-1971) swooped down on the sleeping American troops under the American General Hobart R. Gay (1894-1983) and massacred 500 American soldiers, before then withdrawing.

Realising that he had made a mistake, on 6 November MacArthur, without telling anyone, ordered General George Edward Stratemeyer (1890-1969) to attack the bridges on the Yalu River with 90 bombers. Three hours before the American planes were due to take off, the general and Secretary of Defense George Catlett Marshall was informed of the situation and immediately forbade the operation. MacArthur was not happy, as he was convinced that this was the only appropriate military tactic in that situation. He also thought that the restrictions imposed by Washington were counter-productive and harmful to the American army.

The operation was finally authorised two days later, but the details of the attack were changed and only the Korean bank of the Yalu River could be bombed, apart from the dams which provided electricity to Manchuria. However, Soviet fighter jets were based close to Andong (now called Dandong) in Manchuria and could allow the Soviets to win the battle, insofar as the Western troops could not follow them to their base. MacArthur pointed out this absurd situation to the military staff and demanded permission to enter Chinese airspace, which the President refused out of fear that the conflict would turn into a general war. The Security Council renewed the rule banning the violation of the sanctuary of Manchuria, but authorised another offensive on the Korean bank of the river in order to test China's capacity to react. A few days later, MacArthur sent a message to Washington describing the alarming situation the UN found itself in. He claimed that the Chinese had embarked on an undeclared war, and warned that if no concrete and immediate measures were taken, all hope of success would be lost and a protracted war of attrition would ensue.

At the same time, Wu Hsiu-chuan, the representative of the Beijing government at the UN, was refusing to answer questions about his country's participation in the war, claiming that there had been American aggression in Taiwan. There was therefore no dialogue between the Chinese and the Americans, which made it possible to foresee a larger conflict which the Western nations could not be sure of winning and in which their nuclear power was useless.

The situation was considered dramatic, especially since rumours were circulating that Russia would provide military support to China through its air force if Manchuria were bombed. In addition, during a press conference on 30 November, Truman implied that the Americans were prepared to resort to nuclear weaponry. However, America's allies, foremost among whom was Great Britain, would not support this military tactic. Nonetheless, in spite of the concerns raised by this media appearance by the President, it was unlikely that the USA would drop the bomb. Indeed, the country only had bombs that were the same as, or even more powerful than, those used in Hiroshima and Nagasaki. It was not until the end of 1951 that less powerful bombs designed for tactical use were tested. Consequently, the nuclear weapons that the USA possessed could not be used in Korea because American and Chinese combatants were too close.

On 31 December, a major Chinese offensive was launched: 500 000 soldiers, supported by a large aerial deployment (which was allegedly North Korean but really Soviet), swarmed over Korea and crushed the Western troops, using a Chinese tactic called Hachi Shiki. This involved approaching the enemy in a V-formation which quickly closed around them, while another group passed behind in order to cut off signals, help and reinforcements. On 4 December, the Chinese forces retook Pyongyang, and a month later they retook Seoul. The temperatures, which dropped as low as -35°C, also had devastating effects on the forces involved.

Given the urgency of the situation, the UN was unsure whether to evacuate its troops, but these troops managed to halt the Communist advance. On 15 January, the Americans, under the command of General Matthew Bunker Ridgway (1895-1993), went on the offensive. Seoul was retaken on 14 March and the front stabilised along the length of the 38th parallel at the end of the month, until the armistice was signed.

NEGOTIATIONS AND THE ARMISTICE

From March 1951 onwards, when the situation on the ground was stagnating and sporadic fighting was weakening the forces on both sides, Truman was preparing a project for the declaration of peace which was sent to the allied countries. However, before this document could be published, MacArthur publicly threatened China and issued an ultimatum, without referring the matter to the government. After this, he was relieved of his command and replaced by Ridgway.

While the fighting in Korea was tilting slightly in the favour of the UN forces, the Western powers were faced with two choices:

- Fight until victory. For many observers, this would change the destiny of Asia and the global balance of power between the Western Bloc and the Communist Bloc.
- Accept an armistice with no winner.

Truman wanted to choose the second option, fearing that, if the conflict dragged on, the Soviets would regain their influence in Europe. However, on 22 April, the Chinese launched 34 divisions, eight of which were Korean, to attack the 38th parallel, scattering the South Korean troops in the territory. Even so, Beijing feared serious reprisals from the Americans and forbade General Lui Yalou (1910-1965), the First Commander-in-Chief of the Chinese air force, from attacking UN troops and facilities. As such, the ground offensive on the 22 April lacked aerial support and came to a sudden end. Starting on 27 April, many Chinese soldiers began to surrender, and the Communist front collapsed on 20 May.

At the UN, the Secretary-General Trygve Halvdan Lie (Norwegian politician, 1896-1968) was campaigning for talks between the two camps, but it was not until July 1951 that China agree to negotiate a peace treaty in Kaesong. These negotiations were broken off, then resumed, and interspersed with occasional battles, discussions involving the return of prisoners, and the election of a new American president, Dwight D. Eisenhower (1890-1969). They finally culminated in a military armistice on 27 July 1953.

It was then time to take stock of the situation. After three years of bitter fighting, Kim Il-sung found himself at the head of a country that had been completely devastated: its roads and railway lines had been destroyed, and its factories were no longer operational. An estimated two million North Koreans had fled to the South and the Communist camp was adrift.

The number of Communist soldiers who were killed or wounded in the fighting is shocking:

- 520 000 North Koreans
- 900 000 Chinese.

There were also major losses and casualties among the UN soldiers:

- 843 500 South Koreans
- 136 000 Americans.

However, the people worst affected were the civilian populations. An estimated one million South Korean civilians were killed and there were an estimated two million North Korean civilian victims; some sources put this figure as high as four million.

IMPACT

The Korean War ended where it began, at the 38ᵗʰ parallel. Afterwards, the two Koreas were separated not by a border, but by a demilitarised zone which passes diagonally through the 38ᵗʰ parallel in a 160-mile-long and 2.5-mile-wide strip, making the surface area of the two territories in Korea relatively equal.

NORTH KOREA AND SOUTH KOREA

North Korea rebuilt its economy and industry during the 1950s. During this decade, it had one of the fastest-growing economies in the world, according to sources from Pyongyang. Convinced that the South Koreans would rise up as soon as they had the chance, Kim Il-sung's government regularly sent spies and guerrillas, who were quickly uncovered.

South Korea, for its part, found it more difficult to recover from the war. It was dependent on American aid, the population remained poor, and the years of Rhee's government were marked by cronyism and corruption, until his departure in 1960 following violent student demonstrations.

THE USA AND THE UN

The Americans were mourning their many dead soldiers. Strong anti-Chinese feeling emerged in Washington, which opposed the recognition of Beijing as the government of China, thus preventing it from having a seat at the UN, for

20 years.

The Korean War nonetheless allowed the USA to establish its authority over the Western Bloc and to appear as a country that was ready to go to any lengths to defend its interests and those of its allies. It therefore sent a strong message to its adversaries. The firepower deployed in Korea gave the American giant military credibility and showed the world its ability to react.

The UN proved that it could exist as an armed force, unlike the League of Nations created after the First World War (1914-1918). In addition, its intervention in Korea allowed the UN to legitimise its role as an organisation for peace.

SUMMARY

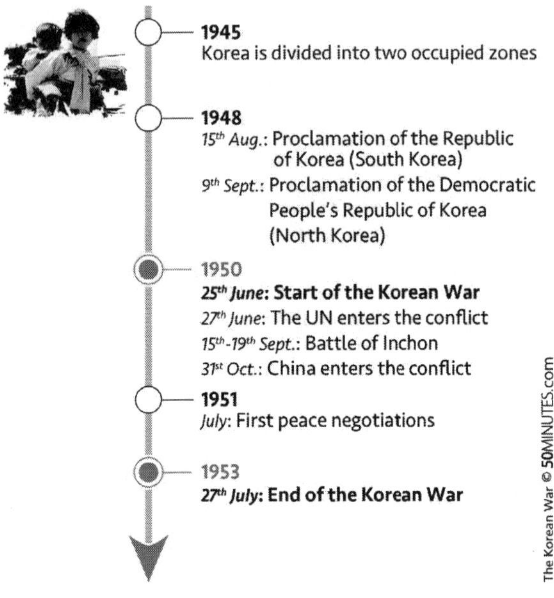

- In August 1945, the Koreans were freed from their Japanese coloniser and had the aim of forming a single great Korea.
- Three years later, after the failure of national elections for the country as a whole, the North, supported by the Soviets, was led by Kim Il-sung, while the South, allied with the USA and the UN, chose Syngman Rhee as its head of government. There were now two Koreas, divided

by the 38th parallel north.

- On 25 June 1950, the North Koreans crossed the imaginary border separating the two countries and rapidly invaded the South of the peninsula.
- Two days later, the United Nations Security Council decided to provide South Korea with military support.
- The Battle of Inchon began on 15 September 1950. In a few days, the Americans took possession of this strategic location and ultimately reconquered the South of the peninsula. However, their armies continued to advance and crossed the 38th parallel on 10 October 1950.
- The Chinese, who felt attacked by the American troops lining their border, reacted on 31 October and intervened in the conflict. After violent clashes, the situation stabilised along the 38th parallel.
- In April 1951, General Douglas MacArthur was relieved of his command by the US president Harry S. Truman for failing to respect hierarchy. He was replaced by Matthew Bunker Ridgway.
- During 1951 and 1952, the Americans and Chinese clashed around the 38th parallel without obtaining any decisive results. Peace talks then began.
- An armistice was signed on 27 July 1953.

We want to hear from you!
Leave a comment on your online library
and share your favourite books on social media!

FIND OUT MORE

BIBLIOGRAPHY

* Cadeau, I. (2013) *La guerre de Corée*. Paris: Perrin.
* Cumings, B. (2013) L'autre scenario. *L'Histoire*, issue 385.
* Dayez-Burgeon, P. (2012) *Histoire de la Corée. Des origines à nos jours*. Paris: Tallandier.
* Delmas, C. (1982) *Corée 1950. Paroxysme de la guerre froide*. Brussels: Complexe.
* Fabre, A. (2001) *Histoire de la Corée*. Paris: L'Asiathèque-maisons des langues du monde.
* Fontaine, A. (1968) *History of the Cold War: From the October Revolution to the Korean War, 1917-1950*. Trans. Paige, D.D. London/New York: Martin Secker and Warburg Ltd.
* Fontaine, A. (1976) *Histoire de la guerre froide. De la guerre de Corée à la crise des alliances*. 1950-1971. Paris: Fayard.
* Hubac, J. (2013) *Dictionnaire chronologique des guerres du xxe siècle*. Paris: Hatier.
* Kersaudy, F. (2003) Une occupation américaine réussie. *Historia*, issue 683.
* Souty, P. (2002) *La guerre de Corée 1950-1953. Guerre froide en Asie orientale*. Lyon: Presses universitaires de Lyon.

ADDITIONAL SOURCES

* Cumings, B. (2011) *The Korean War: A History*. New York: Modern Library.

- Hastings, M. (2010) *The Korean War*. New York: Simon & Schuster.
- Leckie, R. (1996) *Conflict: The History of the Korean War*. Cambridge; Massachusetts: Da Capo Press.
- Salmon, S. (2011) *Scorched Earth, Black Snow: The First Year of the Korean War*. London: Aurum Press Limited.
- Whiting, C. (1999) *Battleground Korea – The British in Korea*. Stroud: Sutton Publishing Limited.

ICONOGRAPHIC SOURCES

- Portrait of Syngman Rhee. Royalty-free reproduction picture.
- Portrait of Douglas MacArthur. Royalty-free reproduction picture.
- Truman giving his signature for the USA's involvement in the Korean War. Royalty-free reproduction picture.
- Portrait of Kim Il-sung. Royalty-free reproduction picture.
- General MacArthur watches the bombardment of Inchon. © US Army.
- American soldiers engaged in a street battle in Seoul in September 1950. Royalty-free reproduction figure.

LITERATURE

- Jin, H. (2005) *War Trash*. London: Hamish Hamilton Ltd.
- Lee, C-R. (2011) *The Surrendered*. London: Riverhead Books.
- Roth, P. (2009) *Indignation*. London: Vintage.
- Sun-Won, H. (2005) *Trees on a Slope*. Trans. Fulton, B.

and Fulton, J-C. Honolulu: University of Hawai'i Press.

FILMS

- *The Bridges at Toko-Ri*. (1954) [Film]. Mark Robson. Dir. USA: Paramount Pictures.
- *Pork Chop Hill*. (1959) [Film]. Lewis Milestone. Dir. USA: Melville Productions.
- *The Manchurian Candidate*. (1962) [Film]. John Frankenheimer. Dir. USA: M. C. Productions.
- *M.A.S.H.* (1970) [Film]. Robert Altman. Dir. USA: Aspen Productions, Inigo Preminger Productions.
- *MacArthur*. (1977) [Film]. Joseph Sargent. USA: Universal Pictures.

Made in the USA
Monee, IL
07 July 2026